About the Publisher

This journal is published by WMAddison Publishing and Greater is Coming Ministries — a ministry founded on one of the darkest days of the global pandemic: December 17, 2020, the day we lost the most lives to COVID-19.

Out of great sorrow came a greater call — a call to reach those who are hurting, grieving, and longing for God's healing presence.

Greater Is Coming Ministries, along with Cooking with Wan on YouTube, was birthed out of pain, grounded in purpose, and fueled by faith.

These platforms exist to remind every soul:

There is still hope.

Greater is still coming.

Through journal reflections, prayers, sermons, cooking and sacred gatherings, these ministries exist to offer spiritual restoration and hope — one heart at a time.

For ministry updates, future offerings, or to connect:

■ *WMAddison2021@gmail.com*

WMAddison Publishing @Greater is Coming Ministries

Table of Contents

Introduction
- About This Book
- Why "Good Grief! I'm Grieving"

Section 1: Shock & Silence
- Stuck, Startled, Shocked
- Unable to Move
- Time Stops

Section 2: The Cry No One Hears
- Crying Isn't Doubt
- I Believe in Heaven, but I'm Still Hurting
- Permission to Grieve

Section 3: A Father's Legacy
- The Journal
- Lessons from Daddy
- "Wanda, I'm Proud of You"

Section 4: Death, Let's Talk

- *Conversations with Death*
- *Assignment vs Emotion*
- *The Cold Consistency of Death*

Section 5: The Grief We Don't Talk About

- *Grieving the Living*
- *Grieving Dreams*
- *Grieving Ministry While Ministering*

Section 6: Family Moments & Sacred Days

- *The Deck Healing*
- *The First Father's Day Without Him*
- *Markers, Not Timelines*

Section 7: The Grief That Lingers

- *Memories and Milestones*
- *The Day I Froze at Work*
- *Waves of Grief*
- *When Grief Swallowed Me*

Section 8: Good Grief

~ *There Is Purpose in Grieving*

~ *Grief as Honor*

~ *Then I Worshipped*

Dedication Page

Dedicated to: John Addison

A Tribute

God Forbid: The Legacy of My Father

From Our Hearts to His

A Family Tribute to Our Beloved

Husband, Father, PopPop

& Great-Grandfather

About This Book

This book was born from pain — and faith.

After the loss of my father, I found myself typing notes on my phone...

raw, unfiltered thoughts about the moments that broke me

and the moments that helped me breathe again.

These reflections became a journal —

and that journal became Good Grief! I'm Grieving.

This is not a manual or a checklist.

It's not a story with a neat ending tied in a bow.

It's a journey. A process.

A sacred, messy, beautiful journey

through the valley of grief...

And toward the God who walks with us in it.

This is a space for honesty.

For tears.

For wrestling.

And for worship.

Why Good Grief! I'm Grieving

The title came to me as both a cry and a confession.

It's an exclamation — "Good grief!"

And a declaration — "I'm grieving."

It means:

This grief is heavy... but it's also holy.

I'm not okay... but I'm also not alone.

This grief is good — not because it feels good,

but because it proves I've loved deeply.

This is grief with God.

This is grief with glory in view.

This is good grief.

Dear Lord,

As I open these pages, I carry the weight of loss,

but also the hope of healing.

Bless the one reading this now.

Meet them in their grief — right where it hurts the most.

Wrap them in Your love and give them space to be fully honest.

Let every word, every memory, and every prayer

be a stepping stone toward peace.

May this book be a companion, a comfort, and a quiet reminder:

you are not alone. You are not forgotten.

And God is not finished.

In Jesus' name,

Amen.

Section: 1
Shock & Silence

~Stuck, Startled, Shocked

~Unable to Move

~Time Stops

~Stuck, Startled, Shocked

Stuck, Startled , Shocked

~Reflection~

This can't be happening...why is the family standing just looking as if this has happened...to gaze upon the faces of the few confirmed it happened..

Everything has gone completely black. Absolutely nothing exists in this moment except darkness and an unbelievable hurt. The tears ,the wrenching screams and cries that have come from the deepest depth of human pain..

Just no ...please not today not now please no....

In this moment it's not about anyone it is not even about God .. it's just hurt devastation depletion..gutted ..crushed

There are moments that feel like still frames in a movie — no motion, no breath, no sound. That's what it felt like. The kind of shock that makes the world stand still and yet spins everything inside you into chaos. I was startled. Startled by what I already knew deep down was coming. And still, I wasn't ready.

I couldn't move. My thoughts were racing and frozen at the same time. Everything and everyone sounded far away. The air was thick with disbelief, like trying to walk through water.

I was startled — not by the event itself, but by my reaction. How do you prepare for your foundation to crack? Even when they tell you it's coming, even when you hear the warning signs… it still hits like a thief in the night.

Shocked that even though I believe in heaven, and I believe in God, my soul still trembled. My flesh still wept. My mind still shouted "no."

And I had to remind myself: this is the beginning of grief. This is the silence before the cry. The holy pause before worship.

This is that silence you get startled into.

Ecclesiastes 3:7 — "A time to keep silence, and a time to speak."

Journal Prompts:

- *When have you felt completely startled in your grief?*
- *What did your mind and body feel like at that moment?*
- *Who or what did you want to reach for — and what did you need?*
- *What would you say to yourself now if you could go back to that moment?*

_____

_____

_____

_____

_____

_____

_____

_____

~Closing Prayer~

Lord,

I didn't expect it to feel like this.

I thought I was prepared, but I wasn't.

I'm stuck — shocked — silent — startled —

and it hurts in places I didn't even know existed.

But I know You are still with me,

even in this frozen space.

You are the God who waits with me in silence.

You are the God who gives me permission to pause.

So even if I can't move today,

help me to breathe.

Help me to trust that You're still holding me,

and that one day — even if it's not today —

I will take the next step with You.

In Jesus' name,

Amen.

~*Unable to Move*

Unable to Move

~Reflection~

I told him it was okay. That was a lie. Everything in me wanted to scream, "Don't go!" But I said, "It's okay" because that's what you say when you want to give peace to someone who's dying...

But it wasn't okay. I collapsed after I said it. I curled up, broken.

Normal vanished for me ...

Am I stuck — frozen, fixed in one place, unable to move?

Am I startled — caught in sudden shock, breath stolen from my chest?

It wasn't getting better.

And of course, reality continued to whisper.

As I tuned in to what I heard.

Everything broke.

Ripped to shreds.

I wanted to take back every word,

but it was too late.

Isaiah 43:2 – "When you pass through the waters, I will be with you…"

Journal Prompts:

- *What did you say during your goodbye — and what do you wish you could say now?*

- *What truth are you still holding back in your grief?*

- *What moment did you realize, "I am not okay"?*

- *How might God hold your honesty?*

_____

_____

_____

_____

_____

_____

_____

~Closing Prayer~

Father, I bring my unspoken truth to You. I bring the parts I couldn't say, the ones I didn't mean, and the ones I regret. Help me grieve honestly — and still trust You in the silence.

In Jesus' name.

Amen.

~*Time Stops*

When Time Stops

~Reflection~

Here I am — not a day, not a month — but a new normal. A lifestyle of living with the feelings, the emotions, and the conditions of this devastating loss...

There are moments when time truly stops. Not just the ticking of a clock — but the rhythm of your life...

Tears fall uncontrollably.

Not once.

Not twice.

But over and over again.

Every tear carries the weight of what I cannot say,

what I cannot bear to hear.

So I stand.

So I sit.

So I lie.

Unable to move forward with time.

Time has stopped.

In this silence,

everything waits.

My body breathes,

but my soul is frozen.

Scripture:

Psalm 34:18 – "The Lord is close to the brokenhearted and saves those who are crushed in spirit."

Journal Prompts:

- *What triggers your emotional shutdown or stillness?*
- *When has grief felt like time stopped completely?*
- *What do you miss most about your old rhythm?*
- *How do you find breath when the weight of grief returns?*

_____

_____

_____

_____

_____

_____

_____

_____

_____

Closing Prayer~

God of Stillness, meet me in this place where time has stopped. Remind me that You are present even here.

In Jesus' name.

Amen.

Section: 2

The Cry No One Hears

~Crying Isn't Doubt

~Believe in Heaven, but I'm Still Hurting

~Permission to Grieve

~Crying Isn't Doubt

Crying Isn't Doubt

~Reflection~

Away from it all is where you want to be,

but life pulls you to stay in the life game.

Keep going — this is not life in its entirety.

It's just a part of it.

I know they had good intentions in helping,

but I couldn't grasp grief according to someone else's title

or according to someone else's position.

That's how you should move. That's how you should cry.

A blot of a tissue is okay — but not a full-blown cry out.

That was for that day. Or for home. But not here.

Do I have to explain each time?

I'm not crying because I have no hope!

or because I don't believe in God.

I understand and believe Heaven is not just a better place —

It's the best place.

But I am in a season of mourning,

and according to the Word of God:

Ecclesiastes 3:1

To every thing there is a season, and a time to every purpose under the heaven:

Even Jesus wept.

So I will honor myself

and allow myself to go through what I need to go through.

I think it's wisdom.

And to whatever title or position you hold —

you have permission to shed the tears ..

While simultaneously believing in God.

Cry. Scream. Be silent.

Do whatever you need to do for yourself to move in a healthy manner forward.

―――

▌*Journal Prompts*

- *Have you ever felt judged for the way you grieved?*
- *What do you wish people understood about your tears?*
- *What does "permission to grieve" look like in your life?*

_____

_____

_____

_____

Closing Prayer~

Dear God,

Some days the tears flow without warning.

Other days I hold them back because I think I should.

Remind me that crying is not a sign of doubt —

It's part of being human.

Even Jesus wept.

Give me the freedom to mourn without shame,

and the strength to trust You through every tear.

Heal the places that hurt,

and help me walk this journey without guilt

for feeling the weight of love and loss.

In Jesus' name,

Amen.

~*Believe in Heaven, but I'm Still Hurting*

Believe in Heaven, but I'm Still Hurting

~Reflection~

Sure, I understand the disease.

Yes, I know this was the process.

And no — I'm not saying I want him to come back.

But I didn't want him to go either.

Not a moment goes by that I don't think about him.

But I've realized something…

This person I now call him

isn't just my dad — he's become him in this season.

Even saying his name crumbles me.

I'm not ready to sit and make jokes.

Not ready to say "remember when."

Not ready to hear his voice in a voicemail or a memory.

I just... am not ready.

The tears fell again.

I didn't even know I had this many tears left in me.

The days are moving on.

But I'm still shattered, shaken, and broken.

I wasn't ready.

Is this really happening?

There are moments when grief actually shows me some mercy —

It exhausts me so deeply that I fall asleep.

Not restless sleep, but deep, peaceful rest.

Grief takes naps, too.

And I've learned I can sleep peacefully beside it.

Grief doesn't leave.

It becomes part of you.

So now I'm different.

Forever changed.

And I must figure out who I am in this new season.

Apparently, there is a way to live together with grief.

But here's the hope:

I found Another who lives inside of me.

I was never alone.

An evangelism opportunity arose — and instantly my insides were leaping.

My emotions were confused, going haywire.

But the Holy Spirit that dwells within me sat grief down for a moment

and reawakened my soul.

I was excited to go.

To toss seeds.

To do the work of the Kingdom.

To lift my head and proclaim that even here —

I am not alone.

Grief may be a part of me now.

But it is not the whole of me.

Galatians 2:20

I have been crucified with Christ. It is no longer I who live, but Christ who lives in me.

And the life I now live in the flesh I live by faith in the Son of God, who loved me and gave himself for me.

Journal Prompts:

- ***What do you believe about Heaven — and how does that affect your grief?***

- ***What emotions are still too raw for you to name aloud?***

- ***Where have you felt the Holy Spirit interrupt your grief with unexpected peace?***

Closing Prayer~

Father,

I know You are with me.

I know my loved one is with You.

But I still hurt.

Thank You for being patient with me as I grieve.

Thank You for the moments where Your presence breaks through.

Even when I don't feel joy — I trust that joy is coming.

And even when I feel broken — I trust that I am still Yours.

Remind me that grief and faith can live side by side.

Because even in my sorrow,

You are my Savior.

Amen.

~*Permission to Grieve*

Permission to Grieve

~Reflection~

I am just in this season of mourning,

and I've come to realize — I don't owe anyone an explanation for how I grieve.

There are titles. There are positions. There are expectations.

But there is also pain. Real, holy, soul-deep pain.

And yes — even Jesus wept.

I give myself permission:

To cry without apology.

To scream if I need to.

To sit silently in a memory.

To collapse when I can't stand.

To be unfiltered, unedited, and fully human in this moment.

This is not faithlessness.

This is faith being refined in fire.

This is grief — holy and heavy.

This is grief — not as a weakness but as a witness.

Ecclesiastes 3:4

A time to weep and a time to laugh,

A time to mourn and a time to dance.

If the Bible says it, why do we act like it's unspiritual to mourn?

No more holding back.

No more hiding tears in tissue corners.

No more edited prayers or empty platitudes.

I give myself — and I give you — full permission to grieve.

LET IT GO.

Journal Prompts:

- *What kind of pressure (spoken or unspoken) have you felt about how to grieve "properly"?*

- *What do you need permission to feel today?*

- *What would it look like to grieve honestly and without apology?*

_____

_____

_____

_____

Closing Prayer~

God,

Thank You for giving me permission to grieve.

Thank You for reminding me that grief does not disqualify me from Your presence —

it brings me deeper into it.

Release me from guilt.

Release me from performance.

Let this grief season be a sacred space

where I can be honest, broken,

and still... deeply loved by You.

I will not hide. I will not rush.

I will not fake peace I haven't yet received.

I will sit with You and be real.

And that will be enough.

Amen.

Section: 3

A Father's Legacy

~The Journal

~Lessons from Daddy

~"Wanda, I'm Proud of You"

~*The Journal*

The Journal

~Reflection~

I didn't know I was writing a Journal.

I was just trying to survive the days.

I typed thoughts into my phone like lifelines — raw, broken, sacred pieces of my pain.

Then one day it hit me:

This grief, these tears, this heartbreak...

It was telling a story.

It was his story.

It was my story.

It was our story — me and my daddy — and God in the center of it all.

This journal isn't a tribute.

It's a testimony.

It's a record of the love I still feel. The faith I'm still clinging to.

It's me, sitting in the valley of the shadow of death —

but deciding to write through it, not just walk through it.

I named this journal Good Grief! I'm Grieving

because that's the tension I live in.

Grief is hard… but grief is also holy.

And this journal— this journey — is proof that even in the most painful places,

God still speaks.

If you're holding this journal, I pray it holds you back.

That somewhere in these pages you find your own story.

That you see your own tears.

That you hear your own voice — and maybe God's voice, too.

Because this journal is more than pages.

It's permission.

It's a process.

It's proof that grief is not the end... and neither is death.

Journal Prompts:

- *What words or phrases would you use to title your grief story?*

- *How has your grief changed or shaped the way you express yourself?*

- *If you could write a letter to someone you've lost, what would the first line say?*

_____

_____

_____

_____

Closing Prayer~

Lord,

Thank You for giving me a voice — even in the silence of sorrow.

Thank You for turning pain into purpose.

Thank You for letting this book be both a cry and a comfort.

Help me write my story with You at the center.

Let every page be honest. Let every tear be healed.

Let this process bring peace — not because it's easy, but because You're in it.

For every person who reads this,

may they find hope in their hurting,

and courage to keep writing their own story — with You.

In Jesus' name,

Amen.

~*Lessons from Daddy*

Lessons from Daddy

~Reflection~

He didn't sit me down at a desk and teach me life with a chalkboard.

He lived it. And I watched.

My daddy was the kind of man who taught by doing —

by waking up early, pressing his shirts just right,

making sure his family was clean, fed, and taken care of.

He was the epitome of strength —

short in stature, but mighty in presence.

They called him Shorty, but his life was anything but small.

I learned how to clean fish, fry chicken, and cook baked beans and fried hot dogs — because Daddy taught me.

No one made grits better than him. No one.

He brought us to church, read his Bible, sang hymns,

and made sure Sunday was God's day — all day.

Choir rehearsal. Prayer service. Bible study.

We watched him live what he believed.

If we were ever poor, we wouldn't know it.

Because wealth to him was togetherness.

Family was his fortune — and he invested deeply.

He loved without fuss, without frills.

He wasn't a hugger, but he showed his love in every sacrifice.

He fixed what was broken. He protected what was his.

And we were his, and we knew it.

He had a way of making everything memorable -

in photography and even his humor.

One day my sisters and I walked in,

and Daddy just looked at us and said,

"Here comes Could've, Would've, and Should've."

We laughed until we cried.

And years later, I reflected — and yep... that was us. ●

He didn't just raise children.

He raised a legacy.

A generation. A family that still feels his fingerprints on everything.

And I'm still learning from him —

every single day.

Journal Prompts:

- *What lessons did your loved one leave behind — spoken or unspoken?*
- *How do those lessons show up in your life today?*
- *In what ways are you continuing the legacy?*

_____

_____

_____

_____

_____

Closing Prayer~

Father,

Thank You for the gift of memory.

Thank You for the love that lingers through every lesson learned.

Even in loss, I am surrounded by legacy.

Help me to carry forward what I've been taught —

to live it, to share it, to honor it.

Let me not just remember...

but also reflect You in all I do,

just like Daddy did.

In Jesus' name,

Amen.

~"Wanda, I'm Proud of You"

"Wanda, I'm Proud of You"

~Reflection~

"Wanda, I'm proud of you."

Just five words...

But they carry the weight of a lifetime.

My father didn't speak for the sake of speaking.

When he said something, you listened.

And when he said that — to me —

it landed deep.

I can still hear his voice,

feel the pause he'd take before saying it.

Sometimes he'd catch me after a sermon or something I'd done,

and with a simple nod, he'd say it:

"Wanda, I'm proud of you."

That meant everything.

Because I knew what it took for him to say it.

He didn't give empty praise —

He gave honest affirmation.

And every time he said it,

I stood a little taller inside.

Not from pride, but from purpose.

Because if Daddy saw it... if he recognized what God was doing in me...

then maybe I really was walking in my calling.

He taught me how to take care of myself —

"Wanda, put oil in that car."

"Don't let your gas run out — fill it up at half."

"Wanda, if you don't have it to give, don't give it. Don't create loans, if it gets returned wonderful."

He reminded me I wasn't a doormat.

He told me he saw my study in the Word.

He cleaned up my tears and my messes.

He prayed for me. And with me.

He saw me. And believed in me.

I will carry those words forever.

On the hard days, the quiet days, the joyful ones —

I still hear them:

"Wanda, I'm proud of you."

And now, through this book...

I hope I'm making him proud again.

Journal Prompts:

- *What is one thing your loved one said to you that you still hold close?*

- *How do you carry those affirmations or instructions with you today?*

- *What words do you want to leave behind for someone else?*

_____

_____

_____

_____

Closing Prayer~

Dear God,

Thank You for the voices in my life that spoke truth and love over me.

Thank You for a father who affirmed me —

not just for what I did, but for who I am.

Let those words echo in my soul when I doubt myself.

Let them remind me that I am seen, loved, and supported — even from heaven.

Use me, Lord, to speak life into someone else the way my Daddy did for me.

In Your name,

Amen.

Section: 4

Death, Let's Talk

~Conversations with Death

~Assignment vs Emotion

~The Cold Consistency of Death

~Conversations with Death

"The days of our years are threescore years and ten; and if by reason of strength they be fourscore years, yet is their strength labour and sorrow; for it is soon cut off, and we fly away".

Psalm 90:10

Conversations with Death

~Reflection~

We sat and had the talk.

My father looked me straight in the eye and said what most people dance around:

"I'm going to die."

He wasn't being mean.

He wasn't being dramatic.

He was being real.

He named everyone in our family and ended with,

"You're going to die too. None of us are going to be here forever."

At the time, it stunned me.

I thought he was being too direct — too heavy.

But now I realize...

He was preparing me.

He had the kind of relationship with death

that only comes from a deep relationship with God.

It wasn't something to fear.

It was something to face.

He faced it with the truth.

With scripture.

With peace.

And now, here I am —

grieving the very man who told me this moment would come.

I thought I was prepared.

I'm not.

I thought the conversation would be enough.

It wasn't.

But I'm still grateful we had it.

Because now I know:

Talking about death isn't giving up on life.

It's honoring it.

And I'll keep talking about it —

not to dwell on dying,

but to live more fully,

love more deeply,

and let others know...

you don't have to be afraid.

Journal Prompts:

- *Have you ever had a conversation about death that stayed with you?*

- *What fears or beliefs do you hold about death — and where did they come from?*

- *If you could say one thing to prepare a loved one in reference to death, what would it be?*

_____

_____

_____

_____

Closing Prayer~

God,

You are the Author of life and the Keeper of every soul.

Thank You for the conversations that prepare us — even if they don't take the pain away.

Help me not to fear death, but to understand it through Your eyes.

Give me peace where there is anxiety.

Give me courage to talk honestly about hard things.

And help me honor those I've loved by how I live.

In Your eternal name,

Amen.

~*Assignment vs Emotion*

Assignment vs Emotion

~Reflection~

Death doesn't care about your calendar.

It didn't ask if I had time to grieve.

It didn't ask if I had finished my to-do list, my ministry work, or my shift at the hospital.

It just... happened.

And suddenly, I was expected to keep going.

Expected to serve, speak, show up, smile.

But the truth?

Grief doesn't pause just because you have an assignment.

And your assignment doesn't stop just because you're grieving.

The two began to crash inside me.

Emotion tugged on my heart.

Responsibility pulled on my back.

I stood in the work place, stood with family, stood in church, stood in meetings, stood —

giving care, giving Word, giving encouragement —

while inside I was breaking in a thousand invisible places.

And yet, I kept moving.

Why? Because somewhere deep within,

I knew my assignment was still alive — even while I was grieving.

But I also learned this:

God isn't asking me to ignore my grief to fulfill my assignment.

He's asking me to bring both to Him.

Because the power of ministry isn't in pretending I'm okay —

It's in showing up with my full self,

tears and all,

and letting Him use it.

That's what Daddy would've done.

That's what Jesus did.

That's what I'm learning to do.

Journal Prompts:

- *Have you ever had to "keep going" in a role while your heart was breaking?*

- *What would it look like to allow space for both your assignment and your emotions?*

- *How can you give yourself permission to grieve while still showing up?*

_____

_____

_____

_____

Closing Prayer~

Lord,

You see every part of me —

the servant and the sorrowing soul.

Teach me to carry my calling with care.

To honor my tears while still honoring the work.

Help me not to perform, but to be present.

Not to hide, but to heal — even while I'm still in motion.

Use my broken places for Your glory.

And let Your strength be made perfect in my weakness.

In Jesus' name,

Amen.

~The Cold Consistency of Death

The Cold Consistency of Death

~Reflection~

Death doesn't flinch.

It doesn't stutter or second-guess.

It doesn't give you a grace period or ask for permission.

It shows up —

on time, every time —

with cold, unwavering consistency.

It doesn't care that I was the daughter.

It didn't soften its blow because I would become shattered.

It didn't pause because we prayed, fasted, believed, hoped.

It just... came.

And even though I knew it was coming —

even though Daddy and I had talked about it —

it still knocked the wind out of me.

There is something cruel about how normal the world remains

after your world has stopped.

People keep walking.

Phones keep buzzing.

Bills still show up.

The calendar flips forward.

But I was still sitting at that moment...

still stuck in the silence...

still watching the door that he would never walk through again.

Death is consistent.

But so is God.

I'm learning that. Slowly.

Death may have been allowed, but it wasn't final.

It didn't win.

It didn't erase the love, the laughter, the lessons, the legacy.

Death arrived with cold certainty.

But God remains with constant presence.

And in the middle of my grief,

I'm holding onto that consistency now.

Journal Prompts:

- *What did you notice most in the immediate aftermath of your loss?*

- *How have you wrestled with the finality of death?*

- *Where have you seen God's presence remain constant — even in grief?*

_____

_____

_____

_____

Closing Prayer~

God of life and eternity,

You are consistent when everything else feels cold and shifting.

Thank You for being present — even when I feel lost.

Even when I'm angry.

Even when the silence is louder than the room.

I don't understand death,

but I trust that You are greater than it.

Help me sit with what's real,

and walk with You as I continue forward —

even if it's one trembling step at a time.

In the name of the One who conquered the grave,

Jesus Christ,

Amen.

Section: 5

The Grief We Don't Talk About

~Grieving the Living

~Grieving Dreams

~Grieving Ministry While Ministering

~Grieving the Living

Grieving the Living

~Reflection~

No one prepares you for this kind of grief —

the grief of people who are still alive.

They're breathing.

They're functioning.

Some are even smiling.

But something is lost.

A relationship fractured.

A connection faded.

A presence that used to feel close now feels far.

And that ache... it lingers.

I sat with tears I didn't even know I had the right to cry.

Because how do you grieve someone who technically hasn't gone anywhere?

What's the funeral for a friendship that died silently?

Where's the memorial for a relationship that's still physically present, but emotionally empty?

This grief is quiet.

It doesn't get hoagie trays, catered meals or sympathy cards.

It doesn't have a name in most circles.

But it lives — inside of us — just the same.

Grieving the living feels like betrayal.

But it's not. It's honesty.

I've learned that you can love someone deeply

and still mourn the space between you.

Sometimes you mourn what used to be.

Sometimes you mourn what never was.

And sometimes, you simply mourn the version of them that no longer exists —

while learning how to still love who they are now.

Journal Prompts:

- *Is there someone you love deeply but feel distant from? What changed?*

- *Have you ever grieved someone who is still alive? What was that experience like?*

- *What kind of healing do you need in those areas of "living loss"?*

_____

_____

_____

_____

Closing Prayer~

Father,

You see the hidden grief — the kind that doesn't have a ceremony.

You know the unspoken losses I carry.

Help me name them.

Help me feel them.

Help me release them to You.

Teach me how to love without losing myself.

And show me how to walk in grace with those who no longer walk beside me.

You are the God who binds up the brokenhearted — even the breaks no one else can see.

In Jesus' name,

Amen.

~Grieving Dreams

Grieving Dreams

~Reflection~

There were dreams I used to carry close.

Dreams of what could've been.

What should've been.

What I thought would be.

Some were big —

careers, platforms, travel, legacy.

Some were quiet —

a phone call, a healing, a normal day without heaviness.

But grief made me realize...

Some of those dreams have quietly died.

And nobody tells you how to mourn that.

The vision you had of your future doesn't match what you see now.

And suddenly, you find yourself sitting in silence with hope that feels half-full.

There are moments I wonder:

Did I fail the dream — or did it just have a different ending?

I don't know all the answers.

But I've come to understand this:

Grieving dreams isn't failure.

It's part of being human.

And even when a dream dies,

God doesn't leave you empty-handed.

He plants new ones.

Sometimes in the same soil.

Sometimes in completely unexpected ground.

But always —

always —

with the promise that he's still writing the story.

Even when it feels like something precious has ended,

God's plans have not.

His Word reminds us

"For I know the plans I have for you," declares the Lord,

"plans to prosper you and not to harm you,

plans to give you a future and a hope."

— Jeremiah 29:11

Journal Prompts:

- ***What dream did you once have that no longer feels alive?***
- ***How have your hopes shifted in this season of grief?***
- ***Are you open to the possibility of God planting something new?***

_____

_____

_____

_____

_____

Closing Prayer~

Lord of my hope,

You know the dreams I held close.

The ones that slipped through my fingers.

The ones that never took shape.

The ones that broke my heart when they didn't come true.

Help me to grieve them with honesty —

not shame.

And give me the courage to believe

that You are not finished with me yet.

That what's ahead may look different —

but it can still be beautiful.

In faith and surrender,

Amen.

~Grieving Ministry While Ministering

Grieving Ministry While Ministering

~Reflection~

I stood while grieving.

There is a weight that comes with serving others while your own soul is shattered.

The expectation to be "strong," to be "available," to keep going —

even when you're the one needing rescue.

The Ministry doesn't pause when you're hurting.

The assignment remains, even when your heart is buried under tears.

And somehow, God still uses your brokenness —

not in spite of it, but through it.

Preaching while silently pleading,

"Lord, please don't let me break down in front of them."

Praying for others while wishing someone would pray for you.

There is a hidden grief in ministry —

a quiet mourning that happens behind closed doors.

Because we're not always allowed to say,

"I'm hurting too."

But I'm learning something:

God never asked me to serve from perfection.

He asked me to serve from presence.

To show up,

to be honest,

and to trust Him with the rest.

Even Jesus wept.

Even Jesus withdrew.

Even Jesus carried grief — and still fulfilled His assignment.

And because He did,

So can I.

Journal Prompts:

- *Have you ever had to lead while grieving? What did that feel like?*

- *What do you wish others understood about your grief in ministry?*

- *In what ways is God still using you, even in your brokenness?*

_____

_____

_____

_____

Closing Prayer~

Father of Compassion,

Thank You for carrying me —

even while I try to carry others.

You see every moment when I show up in tears.

You hear the prayers I whisper silently for myself.

You hold the weight I can no longer bear.

Help me to serve from my surrender, not my strength.

Teach me to rest when needed.

And surround me with those who pour back into me —

as I pour into others.

In Jesus' name,

Amen.

Section: 6
Family Moments & Sacred Days

~The Deck Healing

~The First Father's Day Without Him

~Markers, Not Timelines

~The Deck Healing

Healing on the Deck

~Reflection~

Pushing in the grief...

Then I heard:

"Aunt Wanda?"

That soft voice — the kind voice — of my firstborn niece, Alexis.

Just her presence calmed something in me.

That sweet smile, that warm energy — it helped me breathe differently on the inside.

Then came Taylor — our "mama bear."

Sensitive yet strong. Gentle but fierce.

She loves with her whole heart and helps anyone she can.

Tiffani, our brilliant, vibrant, unapologetic dynamite.

She walks with purpose, speaks with conviction, and doesn't shrink to fit in.

This young woman is a force to be reckoned with.

Jeffrey, the warrior — kind, faithful, and true.

He protects what he loves and only means you well.

And little Amari — one of the three toddlers —

full of energy, full of life.

He just wants to run, play, and watch Paw Patrol , Baby Shark and sing Every Praise.

Together they brought joy like presents under the Christmas tree.

Then came my mother...

Mommy was herself — but different. A little tired.

And it felt different... because he wasn't behind her.

My heart screamed:

"Hold the door open until he comes!"

But he didn't come in.

I had to retreat inward for a moment.

All I wanted was for Mommy to be surrounded — no, engulfed —

in love and laughter so overwhelming that it would hold her together.

Then Renee, my big sister, walked in.

Struggling quietly but showing up strong.

She's the glue. The color.

If I'm the foundation, she's the strength that keeps us all bonded.

And Mark, my brother —

a pillar of strength and love.

Compassionate, committed, and powerful in his presence.

To be his sister means I must stand tall.

Derrick and Tee — light and laughter.

Tee has mastered storms and turned pain into power.

He's a builder, a mentor, a strong example of excellence.

Derrick — my gentle soul. Family-oriented to the core. A snazzy dresser and God-fearing man.

Desiring to capture younger generations into healthy lifestyles — mentally, physically, and spiritually.

Always reminding me he's better at the grill (and truthfully, he is).

But LORD —

IS THE DECK ON FIRE??

What is Uncle Derrick doing out there?!

He has smoked up the entire neighborhood!
●●●

"Shut the deck door before he smokes the whole house!"

We're all dying laughing.

Then comes Aniya, Derrick Jr. (President DJ), and Kaci — arms full of food.

Aniya gives the best hugs.

She doesn't yet realize how priceless she is. A true giver. To know her is to love her to her very core.

Kaci and Amari? A two-person track meet.

Screaming, running, giggling — the house has become a joyful jungle gym.

President DJ (Derrick Jr.) — his embrace fills a room.

This young man is above phenomenal — wise beyond his years and deeply grounded.

Then he joins his dad on the deck, passing plates, grinning from ear to ear.

Even Jasmine, who had to work, made sure her love was felt —

that gentle laugh, those bright eyes, still filling the space.

And last but not least...

My Brandon.

My one and only son.

The one I love deeply and dearly.

He is building a beautiful life in his own way, stepping into fatherhood, and carving his own path.

He has blessed me with my granddaughter, Emani.

When I see her pictures, the joy I feel is unimaginable.

The space in my heart just waits.

I am grateful.

That day — that moment on the deck —

wasn't just about grilled food and laughter.

It was about healing.

It was sacred.

It was family.

It was love finding its way through grief.

Journal Prompts:

- *Who in your family brings you unexpected joy during difficult seasons?*

- *Are there "deck" moments that have helped you feel grounded or comforted?*

- *What does family mean to you in this season of grief?*

_____

_____

_____

_____

Closing Prayer~

God of Generations,

Thank You for moments that remind me joy still lives.

Thank You for family, for laughter, for healing in the small spaces.

Even in grief, You send what I need —

a voice, a hug, a burst of laughter, a plate of food.

Bless my family.

Bless every soul who showed up in my storm.

And help me treasure the sacred days —

even the ones that feel a little incomplete.

You are present in our gatherings.

You are the God of togetherness.

In Jesus' name,

Amen.

~*The First Father's Day Without Him*

The First Father's Day Without Him

~Reflection~

Father's Day.

I never imagined it would feel like this.

Every commercial, every flyer, every reminder was a dagger to the heart.

I didn't go to church.

I didn't want to remember.

But I found myself engulfed, inflamed in memories.

I didn't get cards or gifts.

I didn't make any plans.

I just... remembered.

Remembering the man who made every Father's Day feel whole.

The one who wore his clothes with pride, sat tall in church, and smiled with a quiet confidence.

The one who led our family with strength and humility.

And now?

I sit in silence.

It wasn't the kind of silence that's peaceful —

it was the kind that echoed.

Every photo I glanced at...

Every conversation that danced around his name...

Every quiet tear that fell when no one was looking...

This was the first Father's Day without him.

But I also realized something unexpected that day —

I wasn't alone.

He had left a legacy.

I saw it in the faces around me.

In the laughter of his grandchildren.

In the strength of my siblings.

In the quiet presence of my mother.

In the stories we still told, even through tears.

I heard him.

I felt him.

I honored him —

not just with a card or a gift, but with the life I continue to live.

Grief made the day hard.

But love made it holy.

And somehow, I made it through.

We made it through....

Journal Prompts:

- *What memories surface for you on days like Father's Day?*
- *How do you choose to honor your loved one on significant days?*
- *If you could have them just one more time and could tell them one thing, what would it be?*

_____

_____

_____

_____

_____

Closing Prayer~

Loving Father,

You know the weight of these days —

the ones that shine a light on our deepest losses.

Thank You for the life of the one I miss.

Thank You for every moment we shared.

Thank You that love doesn't die — it continues.

Give me grace for the hard moments.

Give me peace in the quiet ones.

And remind me that even in grief, I can celebrate a legacy.

You are my steady place.

In Jesus' name,

Amen.

~*Markers, Not Timelines*

Markers, Not Timelines

~Reflection~

I kept wondering:

"When will this feel normal again?"

People mean well when they ask how long I plan to grieve.

Some even try to reassure me:

"It gets better after a year."

"The firsts are the hardest."

"Time heals everything."

But the truth?

There's no date on the calendar that signals healing.

No alarm goes off saying, "It's over now."

What I've discovered is this:

Grief doesn't follow timelines — it follows markers.

Like the first time I laughed without feeling guilty.

The first time I heard his favorite song and smiled through the tears.

The first holiday that felt a little less hollow.

These are the sacred markers.

They're subtle, often unnoticed by others, but I see them.

And when I do, I honor them.

Because they don't mean I've moved on —

they mean I'm moving with the memory.

Grief may not end on a schedule,

but God walks with me through every step.

Each marker reminds me that I'm still here, still healing,

and still held.

Journal Prompts:

- *What "markers" have shown you that healing is happening — even slowly?*

- *How has grief changed your relationship with time?*

- *What would it mean for you to release the pressure of a timeline?*

Closing Prayer~

God of Every Moment,

You are not bound by time,

and You do not rush my healing.

Thank You for walking with me —

not just on the milestones,

but in the quiet, sacred markers only You and I know.

Help me to honor the progress I can't always see.

Help me to release the pressure to "get over" anything.

And teach me to rest in the pace of grace.

You are with me — every step, every season.

In Jesus' name,

Amen.

Section: 7

The Grief That Lingers

~Memories & Milestones

~The Day I Froze at Work

~Waves of Grief

~When Grief Swallowed Me

~Memories & Milestones

Memories and Milestones

~Reflection~

It sneaks up on you.

The birthday.

The anniversary.

The song.

The door he no longer walks through.

The chair that stays empty.

The moment when everyone else is smiling and you're forcing your way through it...

because grief showed up — uninvited — again.

I thought milestones would get easier with time.

But it turns out, time doesn't soften all things.

It just teaches you how to carry them differently.

Some days I carry grief in full view —

other days I tuck it quietly in my purse or behind my smile.

But it's always there, waiting to surface at the next memory.

The milestone comes —

and so does the ache.

But now I'm learning to let the ache be holy.

Not something to hide from,

but something to honor — because it reminds me that love was real.

That he was real.

That what we shared didn't end with a date.

I don't rush through the milestones anymore.

I sit with them.

Sometimes I cry.

Sometimes I laugh.

Sometimes I do both at the same time.

Because grief and love — they still hold hands.

Journal Prompts:

- *What milestone or memory catches you by surprise the most?*

- *How do you prepare (or protect) yourself for anniversaries or hard days?*

- *What would it look like to treat the ache as sacred?*

_____

_____

_____

_____

Closing Prayer:

Father of Compassion,

You see the days that come with memories.

You know how they feel before I even speak them aloud.

Thank You for understanding what others might miss.

Thank You for being near when the rest of the world has moved on.

Help me walk gently through these milestones.

Help me honor what I feel.

And help me see how love is still living — even through the ache.

You are my comfort,

and I trust You to hold me when the days are heavy.

In Jesus' name,

Amen.

~The Day I Froze at Work

The Day I Froze at Work

~Reflection~

I was walking through the hallway —

just a regular workday, just doing my job. (ET1)

And then I saw it.

An empty hospital bed.

Parked in the corridor.

Covered in white.

Frozen.

My feet stopped.

My heart did too.

I couldn't move.

Couldn't breathe.

My eyes locked onto the bed as tears filled them faster than I could blink them away.

No one around me knew that I had just stumbled into a memory.

No one saw that, for a moment, I wasn't at work —

I was back in that room.

That day.

That goodbye.

Everything looked normal on the outside.

But inside, I was crumbling.

And then the chairs — the ones with white blankets —

They hit me the same way.

Triggering images of moments I'd been trying to manage, to suppress, to survive.

Was this trauma?

I didn't know.

All I knew was: grief had walked into work with me.

It didn't ask permission.

It didn't knock.

It just showed up, like it always does — loud, invisible, and full of power.

Eventually, I moved.

Eventually, I breathed.

Eventually, I kept going.

But that day taught me something:

Grief doesn't schedule itself around your life — it lives inside of it.

It will come into the workplace, the grocery store, the gas station, the Sunday service.

It will interrupt.

And when it does, you don't have to explain or apologize.

You just breathe.

You just feel.

You just keep walking when you're able.

God walks with you — even when your steps are frozen.

> *Thank you ~ Uzy, Joaquin, Taylor, the A++ team and the entire inpatient pharmacy team. In a time when I was silently unraveling, you helped me in ways that are still unimaginable.* ♥🙏

~~~~~~~~~~~~~~~~~~~~~~~~~~~~~~

Journal Prompts:

- *Has grief ever caught you off guard in a public or professional space?*

- *What helped you move through it?*

- *How can you offer yourself more compassion when the unexpected waves hit?*

Closing Prayer~

God Who Sees,

Even when no one else notices,

You see the tears behind my smile,

the pause in my step,

the memories that hijack my mind.

You never rush me.

You never shame me.

You simply stay with me — even in the frozen moments.

Help me to trust that healing doesn't always look like progress.

Sometimes it looks like stillness.

Sometimes it looks like tears.

But it always looks like You — faithful and near.

In Jesus' name,

Amen.

~*Waves of Grief*

Waves of Grief

~Reflection~

Grief doesn't ask if it's a good time.

It just comes.

Sometimes quietly — a passing thought, a faint memory.

Other times, it crashes.

Loud. Suddenly. Overwhelming.

I could be having a decent day, maybe even a good one.

Then — without warning — I'm drowning.

And I don't always know what triggered it.

A song?

A scent?

A feeling I didn't know was going to arise..

Suddenly, it's all there.

The ache.

The longing.

The weight.

Grief is not a straight line — it's a tide.

It ebbs and flows.

Some days, it just brushes against your ankles.

Other days, it pulls you under.

I used to fight it.

Try to resist the wave.

Hold my breath and push through.

But now?

I've learned to float.

To trust that I won't drown — even when it feels like I might.

To trust that the wave will pass.

And that when it does, God will still be holding me.

I'm not crazy.

I'm not weak.

I'm not mean.

I'm not moody.

I'm just human — deeply, beautifully human.

And grieving....

Grief is part of my humanity now.

Journal Prompts:

- What does your grief feel like when it comes in waves?

- Have you noticed any patterns — times, dates, or triggers?

- What helps you ride the wave instead of fighting it?

_____

_____

_____

_____

_____

Closing Prayer~

Father Who Holds the Storm,

Sometimes the waves feel too big.

Sometimes I forget how to breathe.

Sometimes I'm afraid the tide will never go back out.

But You are greater than the waves.

You speak peace over every flood.

You hold me steady when I cannot stand.

Remind me I am not drowning.

Remind me this is a part of healing, not the end of it.

Help me trust Your arms — even in the undertow.

I float in Your grace today.

In Jesus' name,

Amen.

~When Grief Swallowed Me

When Grief Swallowed Me

~Reflection ~

There are times when you simply cannot get your "Joy factory" to reach authentic joy.

Moments you know — deep down — should be joyful... but you just can't get there. Even with your hardest push, your strongest try, it doesn't come. So you let it go.

You let go of people.

You let go of events.

You let go of the outdoors.

You let go of anything that causes more grief — especially the things you can control — because they block you from accessing your joy factor.

This grief is absolutely too heavy for me to carry anymore.

I have no other choice but to let it go.

Grief takes you deep into itself — so deep it swallows everything about you.

There were days I was crying loudly from the inside...

Help. Help. Please somebody, anybody — help me. I'm dying here.

I experienced even more sadness — possibly even anger — at the fact that no one came.

No one pulled me out.

No one...

Where are they? I wondered. Where are they?

Grief affects you so deeply because of the person — the soul — you loved so deeply.

But it also affects the people around you who actually care. They hurt as you hurt. And they hurt so much, they often don't know what to do... so they do nothing.

Meanwhile, those who mean well — or don't — drop words, assumptions, or expectations:

What they think you should be doing... or not doing.

Those words didn't help. They pushed me further into isolation.

Deeper into grief.

I truly wanted to come out... but I had become my own impossible weight.

Then, Something Shifted

Lo and behold, a bold sister from the Sisterhood — Pam S. — pushed past and lifted me.

And once she did that, it was like the door cracked open. I believe she chipped off something that helped others know: I welcome you.

And slowly...

Marilyn B., Pam W, Bernadette., Monica, Pam H., Kay, Aronissa H., Deb C., Desiree, Cynthia, JuaNita, DeChantal, Tracie E., Penny, Robin A., Tamika C., Yogi ,Tanya, Rhonda, Dimitria .,Kim J., Loretta A., Eric G., JR S., Chandra W., Cheryl H., Valerie R., Renai E., Kari H., Yolanda E., Denise R., Stephanie F., Lisa W., Lynn B.,Dale L., Kim & W. Greg F.,A. Vivian S., Pauline M., Patricia W. and an entire Village (the list was enormous) —

My Pastor Dad, the unmatched Rev. Dr. John Coger, has covered me in prayer and wisdom in ways that words could never fully express. And my New Hope Temple Baptist Church family — wrapped me in love, steadiness, and sacred fellowship. ♥

Every person held pieces of me I didn't even know were scattered.

There was so much support, I couldn't name everyone... but the thought alone brought me to a joyous cry.

Support showed up.

And I discovered something:

Grief took naps when support was near.

And every time support had to leave, I felt a little stronger.

Maybe not healed... but different.

Able to move.

Able to breathe.

I could see sunshine again.

Although grief could have swallowed me,

it had to let me go —

just like Jonah

in the belly of the whale.

~Journal Prompts ~

~What have you had to let go of because it interfered with your ability to access joy?

~Describe a moment when grief felt like it swallowed everything around you.

~Were there people you expected to show up but didn't? How did that affect your healing?

~Who pushed past your silence and reached you?

~When did you begin to see sunshine again? What helped it appear?

~Closing Prayer

God who hears silent cries,
Thank You for being near when I couldn't speak, and when no one came.
Thank You for the Sisterhood — the people You sent to pull me back from the isolation.
Thank You for the church family, for love that didn't need words, for hands that held pieces of me I didn't even know were scattered.
Lord, when grief feels like too much, help me remember You are still here — and so is my village.
Let Your healing shine through the cracks. Let Your comfort rest when support arrives.
And when it's time, let me feel the sunshine again.

In Jesus' name,

Amen.

Section: 8

Good Grief

~There Is Purpose in Grieving

~Grief as Honor

~Then I Worshipped

~There Is Purpose in Grieving

There Is Purpose in Grieving

~Reflection~

At first, I just wanted it to end.

The ache.

The crying.

The way time slowed but never gave me enough of it.

Grief felt like a punishment. A sentence. A dark cloud I couldn't outrun.

But slowly...

quietly...

God began to show me something I couldn't see before:

Grief isn't only about loss.

It's also about love.

You only grieve deeply what you loved deeply.

You only hurt this much because your heart held that much.

I started to realize...

There is purpose in this pain.

Not because God needed me to grieve,

but because He knew that on the other side of it,

I would find a part of myself I didn't know existed.

A version of me that is more compassionate.

More patient.

More prayerful.

More present.

Grief has taught me how to pause.

How to feel.

How to listen to silence.

How to look for God not just on the mountaintop, but in the valley too.

It hasn't been easy.

It still isn't.

But I'm beginning to believe this:

Grief is not the end of the story.

It's part of becoming.

Journal Prompts:

- *What has grief taught you about yourself?*
- *What new depths of faith or strength have you discovered?*
- *Can you find any evidence of purpose in your own grief journey?*

_____

_____

_____

_____

Closing Prayer~

God of Redemption,

I don't always understand why.

But I believe in the who —

You.

The One who wastes nothing.

The One who can bring beauty from ashes.

Help me to see the purpose You are revealing through the pain.

Help me not to rush past what You're showing me.

Use this season to deepen my faith and widen my heart.

I trust that even this — even this — is not wasted.

In Jesus' name,

Amen.

~*Grief as Honor*

Grief as Honor

***~Reflection~*;**

I never thought of grief this way before —

as a form of honor.

But somewhere in the stillness, God whispered it to my spirit:

"You are grieving because you loved well. And that love is still speaking."

Every tear I cry is a testimony.

A sacred reminder that someone lived... and mattered... and shaped my life forever.

Grief is the echo of that love.

It doesn't mean I haven't accepted reality.

It doesn't mean I lack faith.

It simply means — I remember.

I honor my Daddy with every silent pause, every moment I feel his absence.

I honor his life by continuing to live mine with the values he instilled.

I honor him by loving my family, showing up for people, worshiping God, and telling the truth — just like he did.

Grief is love's evidence.

Grief is love's proof.

And in that way, grief becomes something holy —

a way to honor the ones who've gone ahead.

Journal Prompts:

- *In what ways can your grief become an expression of honor?*

- *What values or memories from your loved one do you want to carry forward?*

- *How does remembering them help shape who you are becoming?*

_____

_____

_____

_____

Closing Prayer~

God of All Comfort,

Thank You for the gift of love that was so deep, it left an imprint.

Thank You for the one I grieve — for their life, their legacy, and the love we shared.

Teach me how to honor them in how I live.

Not just with words, but with choices.

Not just with tears, but with growth.

Let my grief become gratitude.

Let my mourning give way to meaning.

In Jesus' name,

Amen.

~Then I Worshipped

Then I Worshipped

~Reflection~

I was breaking down... and nobody could fix it.

Not a counselor. Not a friend. Not a scripture. Not even my own prayers.

I was numb.

Tired.

Gone.

Somewhere in the flood of my sorrow,

a song found me.

And then — in the middle of my breakdown — I heard her voice.

Deaconess Willa Mae. Giving her testimonial song....

She wasn't physically there, but her voice was:

"One day I was burdened, my mind was ill at ease...

I was searching for an answer, and I found it in the tree...

And it whispered saying,

God is the answer, God is the answer, God is the answer —

He's the answer in the time of storm."

She used to sing that with power.

And somehow, my soul started humming along.

With a cracked voice and trembling hands.

No answers — but I had a sound.

No strength — but I had a Savior.

No grand moment.

No platform.

Just grief... and God.

Because worship isn't just for the good days.

It's for the breaking ones too.

as tears ran down my face and my spirit groaned with more than words,

I remembered:

He is still worthy.

Even now.

Even in this.

Worship isn't about a perfect place.

Sometimes it's what happens after the tears.

After the scream. After the silence.

It's the lifting of your heart when your head is bowed low.

It's sacred. It's survival.

*It's the moment when your grief kneels...
and your faith stands.*

It happened ~

I worshipped.

I Worshipped!

I WORSHIPPED......

Journal Prompts:

- *What have you learned about the connection between grief and worship in your own journey?*

- *When was the last time worship surprised you — rising up from a place of pain or uncertainty?*

- *How has the Holy Spirit ministered to you during your hardest moments?*

- *Write a prayer of surrender, or a song of gratitude, even in the midst of your "not yet."*

_____

_____

_____

Closing Prayer:

Precious Holy Spirit,

Thank You for dwelling within me — for guiding me into truth when all I could see was sorrow.

In my weeping, You whispered peace. In my confusion, You anchored me in worship.

God, You are still good — even when grief roars.

You are still worthy — even when I tremble.

You are still near — even when the diagnosis arrives or the loss feels too heavy to carry.

Thank You for teaching me that worship is not about how I feel...

It's about Who I trust. And I trust You.

So I worship.

In grief — I worship.

In joy — I worship.

In every "I don't know" — I worship.

And when I forget, draw me back to You again.

Remind me that I'm not walking this journey alone.

You are here. You always have been.

In the name of Jesus,

Amen.

Dedicated to:

Deacon John Addison

12/14/46 ~ 2/1/25

Tribute
God Forbid:
The Legacy of My Father
A Tribute: Written, Read & Sung
From the heart of
Wanda Michele Addison

God forbid.

I lived a life that brought me joy, peace, happiness—

And yes, some pain that led to wisdom.

I married, produced children...

Who produced children...

Who produced children.

I even saw my great-grands.

My nephews, nieces, cousins, brothers, and sisters—whew.

And even adopted kids.

So proud of my lineage—

Standing tall on their own feet,

Able to prop up their young.

A beautiful wife.

I traveled a lot.

Spent time with family and friends.

Dined in and dined out.

And lest we forget—

God was intertwined in my entire life.

That was the absolute greatest part.

He carried me through the whole journey.

And I couldn't help but pass Him down.

He promised three score and ten—

And look...I passed it.

Call me grateful.

Call me beyond blessed.

But then—

Is it today, yesterday, or tomorrow?

Who are you?

Who are they?

How do I brush my hair?

Wait—I was walking...

Why am I not driving?

What time is it?

Oh—I ate already?

I'm not sure.

Dementia.

What is this?

Impairment of at least two brain functions, such as memory loss and judgment.

You mean—

My brain has forgotten how to tell my body to function?

God forbid.

Should I pretend I don't know these people—

By removing the glitter in my eyes and the smile from my face?

God forbid.

Should I cast the love I have for my Lord

Into a bottle and throw it out?

God forbid.

Should I teach them that all is lost?

God forbid.

Should I not perk up at the sound of my favorite hymns—

As if they only moved my flesh

And not my very soul?

God forbid.

Should I not bow in prayer—

As if this flesh wasn't trained to submit humbly to the Almighty Father?

God forbid.

Should I not run with laughter,

Knowing I'm going to see them again—

As if the house rule was anything but...

"As for me and my house, we will serve the Lord"?

God forbid.

Should I allow my lineage to suffer silently,

Because they think a disease decided for me?

God forbid.

Should I...?

Should I...?

Well, should I is over.

I'm here.

I'm all brand new.

I'm looking to see you all one day—

But if I don't...

God forbid.

———

I had a charge to keep, I had,

A God to glorify,

A never-dying soul to save,

That was fit for the sky.

To serve the present age,

My calling was fulfilled.

O may it all my pow'rs engage—

I did my Master's will.

He armed me with watchful care,

To live always in His sight,

And now, His servant stands prepared

To give account with light.

He helped me to watch and pray,

And still on Him rely.

He never let my trust betray—

But pressed me toward the sky.

Am I a soldier of the cross,

A follow'r of the Lamb?

And shall I fear to own His cause,

Or blush to speak His name?

Must I be carried to the skies

On flow'ry beds of ease,

While others fought to win the prize,

And sailed through bloody seas?

Are there no foes for me to face?

Must I not stem the flood?

Is this vile world a friend to grace,

To help me on to God?

Sure I must fight if I would reign.
Increase my courage, Lord!
I'll bear the toil, endure the pain,
Supported by Thy Word.

Thy saints in all this glorious war
Shall conquer, though they die.
They see the triumph from afar—
By faith's discerning eye.

When that illustrious day shall rise,
And all Thy armies shine
In robes of vict'ry through the skies—
The glory shall be Thine.

———

A Medley of My Father's Favorite Songs

(As sung in his honor)

🎵*I am Thine, Oh Lord, I have heard Thy voice,*

And it told Thy love to me;

But I long to rise in the arms of faith,

And be closer drawn to Thee.

Draw me nearer, nearer, blessed Lord

To the cross where Thou hast died;

Draw me nearer, nearer, blessed Lord

To Thy precious, bleeding side.

🎵 *The Lord is blessing me...*

I can feel His mercy...

As before Him I bow...

I may not be able to see..

All the Lord has done for me...

But the Lord is blessing me ...

Right now, Right now...

🎵 Hold my hand, Lord Jesus, Hold my hand Lord Jesus, hold my hand Lord Jesus....hold my hand....every day every hour let me feel thy cleansing power. Give me power every hour to go through.....

Love you Forever Daddy, Wanda

🌿 *From Our Hearts to His*

A Family Tribute to Our Beloved Husband, Father, PopPop & Great-Grandfather

♥ *Mom – Yvonne Addison*

A mother's love never stops — and yours continues to cover us all.

"There's a saying, 'You can choose your friends but you can't choose your family.'

However, if I could choose my family it would be you.

I am eternally grateful for God's choice for me."

Mommy, we thank you for your unwavering sacrifice. Thank you for the love you continue to demonstrate and give to our family.

John & Yvonne Addison

April 2, 1966 ~ February 1, 2025

♥ *Renee Bundy – Eldest Daughter*

The ache is real, and the words are hard to find — but the love remains constant.

"I just can't seem to put a sentence on paper. My brain just won't allow me.

I just want the days to come when we all can just think of Daddy with joy and always celebrate him."

~Renee, thank you for being more than a faithful daughter. I am proud of the Woman you have become.

♥ *Mark Addison – Eldest & First Son -*

Even joy feels incomplete without you.

"A celebration on this day without you isn't a celebration 💬"

~Mark thank you for walking with me through this journey, not only as my son and friend but as a Man of faith and honor. You have made me beyond proud.

♥ **Derrick Addison – Youngest Son, "Baby Boy"**

Grief reshapes life — but love like yours remains unshaken.

"Pop!! It's just different. We love you."

~Derrick thank you for your steadfast spirit, for your comfort and showing up as a Man honoring God. I am also proud of you.

♥ Grandchildren Tributes

♥ 1st Grandchild — Brandon Hurst

Brandon, the first grandchild, carries quiet strength and compassion. His presence brings peace, and his heart remains deeply connected to his grandfather.

"It's not a moment that goes by that I don't think about PopPop."

♥ **2nd Grandchild — Alexis Addison**

Alexis, deeply thoughtful and tender-hearted, holds sacred memories of PopPop.

"Every time I go to type a sentence about you it brings me to tears and I just can't find the words, I love you pop pop ♥"

Thank you, Alexis, for loving him with a tender heart and honoring him even when the words won't come.

♥ **3rd Grandchild — Jeffrey Bundy, Jr.**

Jeffrey carries PopPop's strength with quiet determination.

"I just can't let him go ....."

Even in silence, love speaks. Thank you, Jeffrey, for showing us that holding on doesn't mean you're not strong — it means you loved deeply.——

4th Grandchild — Taylor Bundy

"You were my strength when I had none, my comfort without asking.

Because of you, I learned how to endure,

how to love deeply,

and still hold myself together.

I miss you every day, Poppop."

Taylor, your heart reveals the depth of his love and the legacy of endurance he placed in you. Thank you for showing us what strength looks like through grief.

♥ **5th Grandchild — Tiffani Bundy**

"The kind of PopPop who drove me to school every day & stopped for breakfast to tour Temple's campus even if I was late... is the PopPop I had.

Oh how I miss those life talks over a breakfast sandwich..."

Tiffani, thank you for reminding us that love often shows up in the simple moments — the talks, the rides, the presence.

♥ **6th Grandchild — Aniya Addison**

"PopPop aka my Donald Duck... my heart... the one who loves hard but always so gentle.

Smiling, humming, tapping your feet... every day just wishing I could hug you one more time or even just hand you the brush you always asked me for.

I love you and miss you... a lot."

Aniya, thank you for sharing your sacred memories. His tenderness lives on in your love.

♥ **7th Grandchild — Jasmine Addison**

"Oh how blessed I was, on the day of Kaci's Dedication... to have you there smiling, giving your warm embrace, my dear PopPop.

Always quiet... yet... I always felt you here & I still do."

Jasmine, thank you for sharing your heart. His quiet strength lives on through you.

♥ **8th Grandchild — Derrick Addison, Jr. (DJ)**

"PopPop, your tenacity shows up in each and every single person within this family.

Your impact is heard, seen and felt all throughout everyone and is what makes us strong!!"

DJ, thank you for honoring him with your life and your strength. You are living proof of his powerful influence.

♥ Great-Grandchildren Tributes

♥ 1st Great-Grandchild — Kaci O.

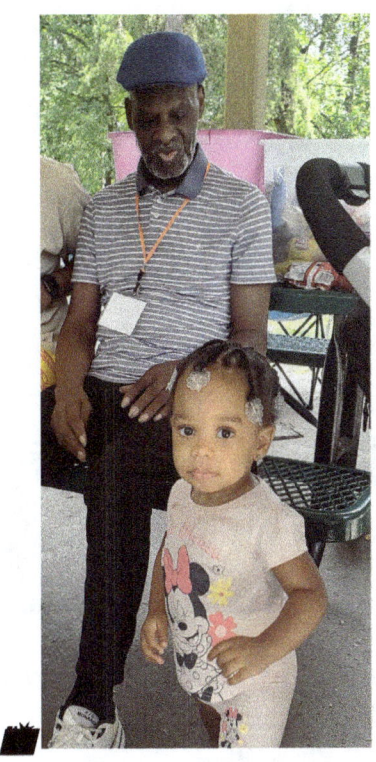

Loved unconditionally by PopPop.

A quiet strength. A sweet spirit. A joy to our hearts.

"Your eyes always found me. Your love will always follow me."

2nd Great-Grandchild — Amari P.

PopPop's energetic shadow — always moving, always exploring.

"Your little buddy. I'll grow up learning your big legacy."

Amari, you carry a spark of PopPop's vibrant spirit. Your joy is a gift to all of us — and your actions are a promise to carry his legacy forward.

♥ *3rd Great-Grandchild — Emani H.*

PopPop's sweet girl.

Though she's still growing, we will make sure she knows the depth of your love.

"I didn't have long, but I had love. And that's forever."

"Forever Changed"

"I guess grief already knew........

I just needed to catch up with the reality."

The end...

And repeat until...

Father,

This journey is not finished.

Some days we walk. Other days we crawl.

But I'm still here — and You are too.

Help us to give ourselves grace in this process.

Remind us that healing doesn't follow a calendar.

And even when we feel stuck, You are still moving within us.

Hold us until we can lift our hands again.

Sit with us until we can sing again.

And love us until we can feel joy again.

We trust You with the parts of us that are still unraveling.

And we thank You for never rushing us through our grief.

In Jesus' name,

I offer all my prayers with Thanksgiving.

Amen.....

 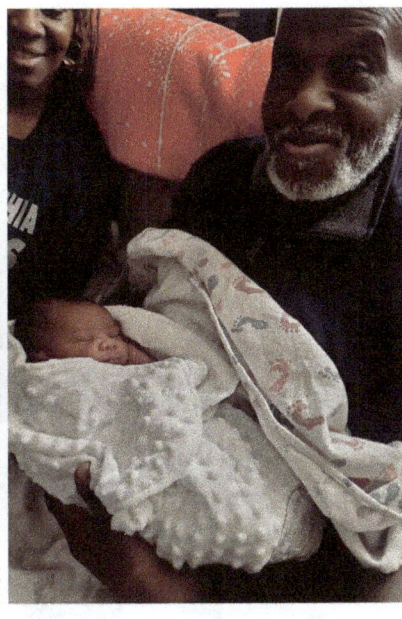

Rev. Wanda Michele Addison is a lifelong member of New Hope Temple Baptist Church where she serves as one of the Directors of Youth Services, a teacher in the School of Discipleship, and Director of the Ministry to Women. She received her license to preach on August 2, 2015, and was ordained on February 10, 2024. She is the current President of the Women's Ministry for both the Pennsylvania Eastern Keystone Baptist Association and the Pennsylvania Baptist State Convention Eastern Region. She has worked in pharmacy for over 25 years. She graduated Summa Cum Laude in Biblical Studies~ Theological Seminary on May 24, 2019. She is the mother of one son, Brandon, and grandmother ("MomMom") to Emani Brielle. Her favorite scripture is

But seek first the kingdom of God and His righteousness, and all these things shall be added to you. Matthew 6:33.

To God be the Glory for the Things He has done.

www.ingramcontent.com/pod-product-compliance
Lightning Source LLC
Chambersburg PA
CBHW070641160426
43194CB00009B/1532